Rain Forest
HABITATS

BY ARNOLD RINGSTAD

Published by The Child's World®
1980 Lookout Drive • Mankato, MN 56003-1705
800-599-READ • www.childsworld.com

Acknowledgments
The Child's World®: Mary Berendes, Publishing Director
Red Line Editorial: Editorial direction
The Design Lab: Design
Amnet: Production

Photographs ©: Dr. Morley Read/Shutterstock
Images, cover, 1; Shutterstock Images, back cover,
5, 6–7, 12–13, 15, 16, 18–19, 23; Eric Isselee/
Shutterstock Images, back cover; Anton Ivanov/
Shutterstock Images, 8–9; Banana Republic
Images/Shutterstock Images, 10; Digital Vision, 21

ISBN 9781623239916
LCCN 2013947271

Printed in the United States of America
Mankato, MN
December, 2013
PA02192

Table of Contents

Welcome to the Rain Forest!

Rain forests are only a small part of Earth. But they have many plants and animals. Rain forests have warm weather. It also rains a lot in rain forests. Many kinds of animals live there. More than half of all known animal **species** live in rain forests. Many of them live nowhere else in the world.

Animals and plants in rain forests work together to live. Animals use trees as food and housing. Some animals eat seeds and fruit. This spreads seeds to new areas. **Predators** help control **populations** by eating other animals.

Deforestation puts the world's rain forests in danger. It is dangerous to plants and animals. People cut down trees to make new roads or build farms. But this destroys habitats.

Thick treetops cover the amazing plant and animal life in the rain forest below.

Where Are the World's Rain Forests?

All of Earth's rain forests are near the **equator**. This location gives them plenty of warmth and sunlight. The plants and animals of the rain forest need this to live.

The world's largest rain forest is the Amazon. It is spread across nine countries in South America. Most of the Amazon is in Brazil. The Amazon has more species than any other rain forest.

Other major rain forests are in central Africa and southeast Asia. A large African rain forest is in the

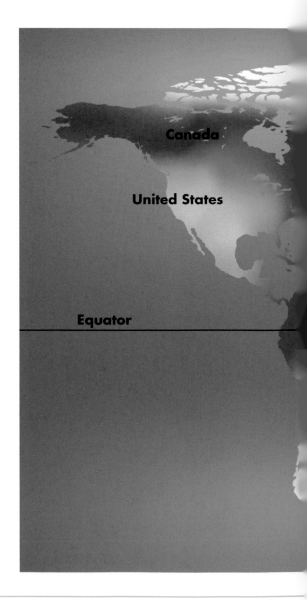

Rain forests can be found across the world in countries near the equator.

Democratic Republic of the Congo. Another is on the island of
Madagascar. Many southeast Asian rain forests are in India
and Indonesia.

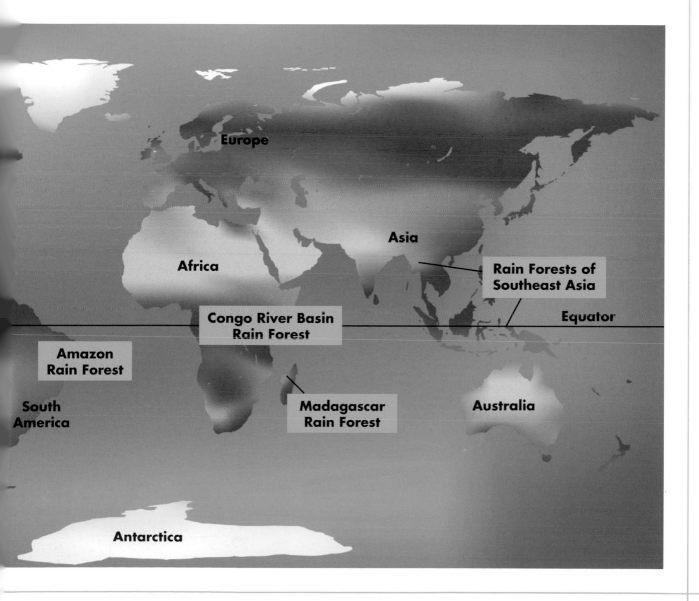

Europe

Asia

Africa

Rain Forests of
Southeast Asia

Congo River Basin
Rain Forest

Equator

Amazon
Rain Forest

South
America

Madagascar
Rain Forest

Australia

Antarctica

What Do Rain Forests Look Like?

Rain forests are filled with life. The tallest trees reach more than 200 feet (61 m) high. Smaller trees and other plants reach 65 feet (20 m). The tops of these trees and plants make up the **canopy**. The canopy blocks sunlight from reaching the ground below.

The plants below the canopy must be able to live in shade. These plants are widely spread out. Their area is called the **understory**. Below the understory is the forest floor. Leaves and twigs cover the ground. They are food for small animals. Few plants grow here.

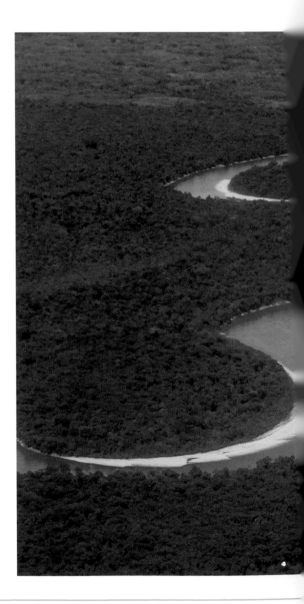

Many animals and plants call the Amazon River home.

Rivers sometimes run through rain forests. One of the most famous is the Amazon River. It runs through the Amazon rain forest. The Amazon River is one of the world's largest rivers.

The Amazon River is about 4,000 miles (6,437 km) long. It can be up to 120 miles (193 km) wide.

Warm and Humid

Rain forests do not have seasons. This is because these forests are near the equator. There is an even amount of sunlight all year. In the United States, daylight gets longer in the summer. But in rain forests, daylight stays the same length all year. The sun makes it easy for plants to grow.

The temperature in rain forests stays about the same all year, too. It is usually between 68 and 77 degrees Fahrenheit (20 and 25 degrees Celsius).

You might guess that rain forests get a lot of rain. You would be right! Rain forests usually get more than 100 inches (254 cm) of rain each year. The canopy keeps this water inside the forest. This makes the understory very humid.

Rain forests are filled with sunshine most of the year.

Plants of the Rain Forest

The biggest plants of the rain forest are the trees. One kind of tree in the Amazon rain forest is the kapok. It can grow 200 feet (61 m) tall and 10 feet (3 m) wide. Many plants and animals live in its holes and branches. Bats like the flowers of the kapok tree. These bats help spread the trees' **pollen**.

The giant water lily also grows in the Amazon. It looks like the lily pads you might see in a pond. But these lily pads are huge. They can be 8 feet (2.4 m) across. An adult can sit on one and it would still float.

The world's largest tropical flower grows in Indonesia. This plant is

Giant water lilies grow in clumps in the Amazon River.

called the titan arum. Its leaves can grow up to 20 feet (6 m) tall! The flower smells like rotten meat or eggs. Insects like this smell. When insects fly into the flower, they help spread its pollen.

Living in the Trees

Many animals live in rain forest trees. The sloth lives in South America. It spends most of its time in tree branches. People might think sloths are lazy. They sleep most of the time and move very slowly. Sloths are specially **adapted** to living in trees. Sleeping and moving slowly helps save energy. Their special stomachs give them lots of energy from the leaves they eat.

Some orangutans' arms stretch out to reach almost 8 feet (2 m) long.

Orangutans make their nests in Indonesia's rain forests. They sleep in a new tree nest each night. Orangutans have very flexible lips. This lets them make more faces than any other ape. They eat fruits that grow in the rain forest. This helps spread seeds.

The macaw is a large, colorful bird. It lives in the rain forests of Central and South America. Its powerful beak lets it eat the food it likes. Macaws use their beaks to crack open nuts. When they eat these, they spread seeds in the rain forest.

Macaws can be many different colors. Red, blue, and yellow are common macaw colors.

On the Rain Forest Floor

Rain forest animals do not just live in the trees. Many also live on the forest floor. One major predator in the Amazon rain forest is the jaguar. These large cats control animal populations by eating other animals. Humans are the only predators of jaguars. No animals hunt these large cats.

Pink river dolphins live in the Amazon River. They eat many kinds of fish. Another animal of the Amazon River is the giant river otter. Sometimes the otters and dolphins work together to hunt fish.

Army ants live on rain forest floors in South America, Africa, and Asia. They live in huge groups of up to 700,000 ants. Sometimes the groups kill lizards or snakes. However, the ants do not eat them. Birds follow the ants and eat the leftovers.

A scary snake lives in rain forests in Southeast Asia. It is the king cobra. It can grow 18 feet (5.5 m) long. The king cobra's poison can kill people and animals. Angry cobras can raise their heads 3 feet (1 m) off the ground. Then they chase their enemy.

An angry king cobra lifts its head off the ground.

The Fierce Piranha

The piranha lives in the streams of the Amazon River. It has sharp teeth and grows up to 18 inches (46 cm) long. Some people try to catch piranhas to eat. But this can be hard to do. Their teeth can cut through fishing lines.

The piranha controls populations. It eats many other kinds of fish. It hunts in groups of up to 30 fish. Sometimes piranhas kill their own prey. They also eat food leftover from other predators. Piranhas sometimes eat plants, too.

Piranhas are known for being fierce. In 1914, President Theodore Roosevelt started a legend about the fish. He went hunting near the Amazon River. He said he saw piranhas eat a whole cow in just a few minutes.

Piranhas may not look scary, but they have long, sharp teeth.

However, this is not normal. Roosevelt's guides wanted to impress him. They put hundreds of hungry piranhas in the water. This does not happen in the wild.

Threats to the Rain Forest

Rain forests are beautiful places. They have many plants and animals. But today they are in danger. The biggest threat is deforestation. Deforestation happens for many reasons.

Some farmers cut down the trees of the rain forest. This clears land for crops and farm animals. Cutting down trees is harmful to the rain forest, however. It destroys the habitats of many plants and animals. When animals die, they cannot spread pollen or be food for other animals. Deforestation harms animals all over the rain forest.

Governments cut down rain forests to make room for roads. This makes a new danger for animals. They may be hit by a car or truck. Pollution from cars also hurts plants and animals. However, people can save the rain forest habitats. People can tell their governments to make laws against deforestation. Humans must take care of rain forests so they will be safe homes for plants and animals.

Too many rain forest trees are being cut down. This harms the habitat.

GLOSSARY

adapted (uh-DAPT-ed) Animals have adapted when they have adjusted to their habitat. Sloths are adapted to living in trees.

canopy (KAN-uh-pee) The branches and leaves of treetops are called a canopy. The rain forest canopy gives shade to the ground below.

deforestation (dee-FOR-ist-ay-shuhn) Deforestation is cutting down trees to clear land for other uses. Deforestation is a danger to rain forests.

equator (i-KWAY-tur) The equator is the imaginary line around the Earth that is an equal distance from the north and south poles. Rain forests are near the equator.

pollen (POL-uhn) Pollen is a powder that helps plants reproduce. Many rain forest animals spread pollen.

populations (pop-yuh-LAY-shuhns) All of one kind of animal that lives in an area is a population. Predators help control animal populations.

predators (PRED-uh-turs) A predator is an animal that hunts and eats other animals. Jaguars are predators.

species (SPEE-seez) A species is a kind of plant or animal. The Amazon has more species than any other rain forest.

understory (uhn-dur-STOR-ee) The understory is the area below the treetops of the rain forest. The canopy is above the understory.

TO LEARN MORE

BOOKS

Kalman, Bobbie. *A Rainforest Habitat*. New York: Crabtree, 2007.

Levinson, Nancy Smiler. *Rain Forests*. New York: Holiday House, 2008.

Simon, Seymour. *Tropical Rainforests*. New York: Harper Collins, 2010.

WEB SITES

Visit our Web site for links about rain forest habitats:
childsworld.com/links

Note to Parents, Teachers, and Librarians: We routinely verify our Web links to make sure they are safe and active sites. So encourage your readers to check them out!

INDEX

ABOUT THE AUTHOR

Arnold Ringstad lives in Minnesota. He likes to visit the local zoo so he can see animals from all kinds of habitats.